To my mom, what burped me

—A.B.

To all the kids (and kids at heart)
who appreciate a good fart joke

—P.T.N.

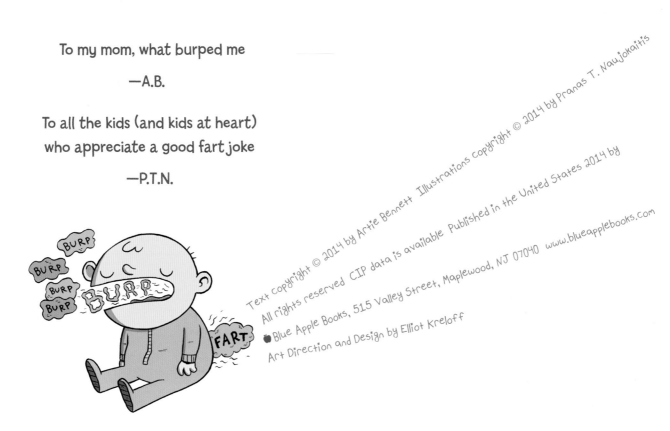

Text Copyright © 2014 by Artie Bennett Illustrations copyright © 2014 by Pranas T. Naujokaitis

All rights reserved CIP data is available Published in the United States 2014 by

🍎 Blue Apple Books, 515 Valley Street, Maplewood, NJ 07040 www.blueapplebooks.com

Art Direction and Design by Elliot Kreloff

First Edition
Printed in China
ISBN: 978-1-60905-392-5
1 3 5 7 9 10 8 6 4 2
08/14

Artie Bennett

BELCHES, BURPS AND FARTS

OH MY!

illustrations by Pranas T. Naujokaitis

BLUE APPLE

Sip or glug or swig or slurp.
Soda's pop will make you burp!
The fizzy gas that gives us joy
Makes burpers of each girl and boy.

Burps are sometimes barely heard

Or loud as any mockingbird!

Here's one of nature's stranger facts:

We cannot burp while on our backs!

Talk too much when chomping chow?

You'll be belching like a cow.

Belch in China? It's not rude!

It tells the chef, "I *love* your food!"

Every living person farts:

All must fart—it's nature's way.
We all "break wind" both night and day.

Though girls will fart as much as boys,
Boys brag more about the noise!

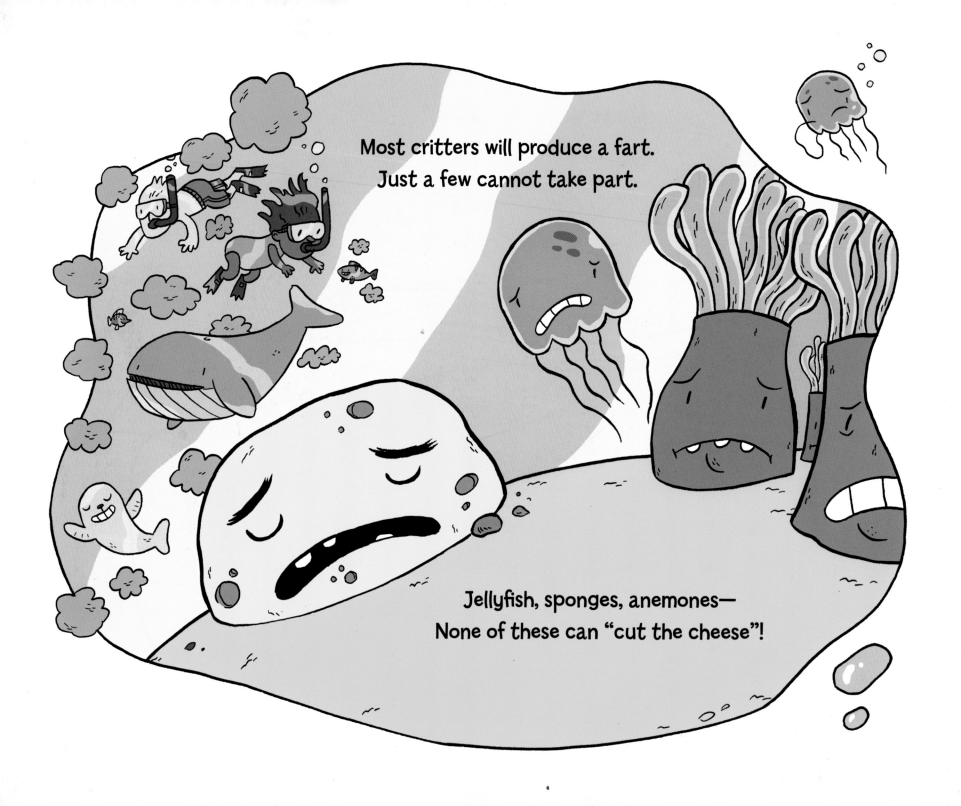

Most critters will produce a fart.
Just a few cannot take part.

Jellyfish, sponges, anemones—
None of these can "cut the cheese"!

Who farts the most? Big surprise! The mightiest is mini-size.

From all the wood that termites chew, they far out-fart the cow or gnu.

Snakes "cut one" to drive away
A predator in search of prey.

Fish fart to communicate.
The bubbles help them congregate.

Lonely beetles need a mate.
Tooting draws a candidate!
A chemical within each fart
Helps to win a beetle's heart!

Dogs fart with alarming ease.
Smell it wafting on the breeze.

Onions, cabbage, turnips, beans
Turn us into fart machines.
Sugars in these foods are tough.
We just can't break them
down enough.

Microbes play a crucial part
In causing us to belch-burp-fart.

Sulfur gives our farts
their smell—
That skunky funk
that we expel.
A veggie such as cauliflower
packs a punch
of P.U. power!

TOOT

TOOT
TOOT

Farts escape when we're at rest.
A bedtime fart can't be suppressed.

And if your room is sealed up tight,
The fart may linger overnight.

PBBBBTT

In closed spaces, wait till later.

Don't rip one in the elevator!

Do *you* fart often? The facts say
We average fourteen toots per day!

There are farts that clear a room,
Even when they don't go "BOOM!"

Watch as all your friends depart
The famed silent-but-deadly fart!

- The word "fart" comes from an Old English word, *feortan*. Experts say that *feortan* was meant to spell out what a fart sounds like.

  - Farts are intestinal gas. This gas comes from swallowed air that gets mixed with intestinal fluids, bacteria, and stomach acid. All combine in varying amounts to make a brew of pure P.U.!

- The scent of gas comes from hydrogen sulfide and other sulfur-containing components. Foods that have a lot of sulfur are cauliflower, eggs, and meat. All yummy (well, maybe not cauliflower), and all very stinky fart-producers!

  - Beans, bread, milk, raisins, cabbage, corn, and peppers are other fart-producing foods for most people.

- The longer you hold in a fart, the smellier it becomes. A withheld fart will absorb other gases before it finally passes.

  - The silent-but-deadly fart is a particularly stinky fart that arrives without any obvious noise. These are farts that tend to have more bacterial contribution and emerge as smaller, warm-and-smelly bubbles. No sound is needed to mark the arrival of an SBD fart!

- Humidity, temperature, wind speed and direction—these are all factors that determine how fast and far a fart will travel. Just ate a big bowl of cauliflower or a batch of eggs for breakfast? Hope and pray for a windy day and try to avoid elevators, small rooms, and car rides!

  - It takes about 13 to 20 seconds after it emerges for us to smell a fart. After that, farts aren't detectable for very long—just a few seconds for most of them.

- The term "morning thunder" refers to a particularly loud fart made soon after waking up.

  - A person can buy special underwear meant to absorb the smell of a fart. It is cheaper, though, just to walk away quickly or blame the dog.

- The official medical term for farting is "flatus."

  - A "whoopee cushion" is a rubber device (resembling a hot-water bottle) that makes a fart-like sound when sat upon. Pranksters hide it under a cushion as a gag.

- Dogs and cats + meat-rich diets = stinky pet farts!

  - Cows + lots of air for digestion = hours of noisy farts!

BURP-TACULAR BITS

- Farts are colorless, but they have inspired these colorful expressions: air attack, backdoor trumpet, bottom burp, Bronx cheer, cheek beep, colon cologne, cut the cheese, Dutch oven, let one rip, ringtailed roarer, step on a duck, talking pants, tooter, and whoever smelt it, dealt it.

  - Where do farts go? Fart gas mostly becomes part of the air or atmosphere of the area where the fart emerged.

- Burps come from the stomach. Farts come from the intestine. Burp gas is different than fart gas. Thank goodness!

  - What's the difference between a belch and a burp? Belches are generally stronger (in noise, force, duration) than burps. You would never belch the baby!

- Burp gas is fast! Burps travel a shorter, less complicated route to their exits than farts. It's stomach to esophagus to mouth to *brrrp!* There usually isn't enough time to cover your mouth before a burp shows up—but you can still say "Excuse me!" after the fact.

  - If you want to burp the alphabet—or your favorite song—you'll need to gulp in a lot of air first.

- If the gas could be collected, the burps of ten cows over a year's time could heat a small house for an entire year.

  - The loudest recorded burp is greater than the roar of a motorcycle!

- Because of the lack of gravity, a burp made while in outer space is likely to bring up some food as well. This is called a "wet burp."

  - The sound of a burp comes from the passing gas causing a small piece of cartilage that covers your windpipe (called the epiglottis) to snap and vibrate.

- A burp is mostly oxygen and nitrogen. Drinking soda adds carbon dioxide to the burpy mix.

  - The official medical term for belching is "eructation."

- Other words for burps and burping: organ recital, air biscuit, soda fart, gas-pression, reviewing the day's menu, belly bark.

Parting advice:
It's better to urp a burp and bear the shame
Than squelch a belch and bear the pain.